All About Animals
Turtles

By Christina Wilsdon

Reader's Digest Young Families

Contents

Chapter 1
A Turtle Grows Up

Turtle Senses

All turtles have good eyesight and an excellent sense of smell. Their hearing is good too.

Mama Turtle swam toward the edge of the pond on a warm night in early summer. She crawled onto the sandy shore. Soon she found the place she was looking for—she came to this nesting ground every year to lay her eggs. Mama Turtle herself had hatched here long ago.

Mama Turtle scraped at the damp, sandy soil with her hind legs. She scooped away sand until the nest was about 5 inches deep.

When Mama Turtle finished digging, she put her tail end into the nest. Then she began to lay her eggs. When she was done, the nest held ten soft, white, oval eggs. Each egg was about an inch long.

Mama Turtle carefully covered the eggs with sand. She smoothed the sand over the nest with her wide, flat body. Then she went back into the water. She did not need to take care of her eggs or the babies that would hatch from them. Her job was done!

The next day, the sun shone on the nest, warming the sand and the eggs. The damp, warm sand also kept the eggs moist. Inside the eggs, the baby turtles grew.

Turtles Are Reptiles

A turtle is a reptile with a shell. A reptile is a cold-blooded animal, which means that the temperature of its body is controlled by the temperature of the air or water around it. Reptiles crawl along the ground or walk on short legs. Snakes, lizards, and alligators are reptiles.

After ten weeks, the eggs were ready to hatch. Baby Turtle was the first to appear. She jabbed at her eggshell with her snout. Then she pushed the egg open with her head and front legs. Right away, Baby Turtle headed for the pond. Luckily, no hungry birds or other animals spotted her.

Splash! She slipped into the water. She paddled around the water plants growing near the shore. Baby Turtle was only about the size of a quarter, so the plants looked like trees to her!

Tiny insects and snails lived among the plants. Baby Turtle did not need to be taught that insects and snails were food. Without even thinking, she snapped up these tasty snacks.

Baby Turtle also knew be on the watch for danger. A shadow on the water could mean a hungry bird was over the pond, ready to snatch up a tiny turtle. A flash of silver nearby could be a hungry fish on the prowl. Raccoons, snakes, big frogs, and crows also liked to eat little turtles.

When Baby Turtle was a few days old, she lost the bump on her snout that had helped her to hatch. This made her look a little bit more like a grown-up turtle. But she was more brightly colored than a fully grown turtle. She also had a ridge in her shell that an adult turtle does not have.

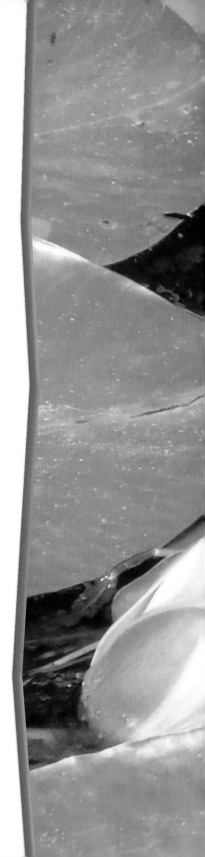

Breaking Out!

A baby turtle has a sharp bump on the end of its snout. When it is ready to be born, the baby jabs this bump against the inside of its eggshell to crack an opening. It's no wonder this special bump is called an egg tooth!

They're Everywhere! Turtles can be found living on every continent in the world except Antarctica.

Baby Turtle did not pay much attention to other turtles she saw in the pond. She joined them only when she wanted to lie in the sun and soak up its warmth. Then she would climb onto a rock or log crowded with other turtles.

Baby Turtle ate slugs, snails, and insects at first. As she grew, she also caught tiny fish, such as minnows. She ate crayfish and the tadpoles of frogs too.

She also began to eat plants. Baby Turtle used her sharp, hard jaws to break apart leaves and flowers. She also liked to eat the green scum, called algae, that grew on the pond's surface.

At night, Baby Turtle rested underwater on the soft mud at the pond's bottom. There she was able to soak up oxygen from the water through some patches of her skin—just enough to keep her alive as she dozed.

It took Baby Turtle six years to grow into an adult turtle. During this time, her colors became a little less bright. The ridge down her back disappeared, and her shell became flat and smooth. Baby Turtle also grew much larger! Her shell was about 6 inches long.

Baby Turtle was now ready to find a mate. Then she would lay her own eggs for the first time—at the same place on the shore where she had hatched.

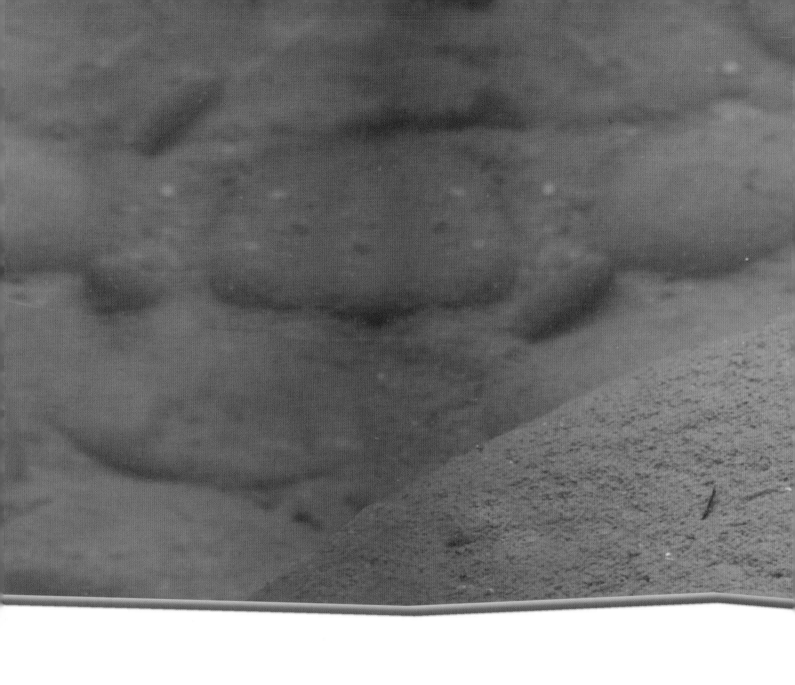

Chapter 2
The Body of a Turtle

The special hinges on this box turtle's shell allow the turtle to close its shell into a tight "box" that no animal can open.

Wild Words

The top part of a turtle's shell is called the **carapace** (pronounced KEHR uh pace). The bottom part is called the **plastron** (pronounced PLASS trun).

A Turtle's Shell

A turtle's shell has two parts—a rounded part on top and a flatter part on the bottom. Both parts are made of bony plates that are connected to each other. With most turtles, these plates are also connected to the backbone, ribs, and other bones inside the turtle's body. The plates are covered with very tough, protective shields called scutes (pronounced *SKOOTS*). The two parts of the turtle's shell are attached.

The shell is a turtle's suit of armor. Many kinds of turtles can fold or pull their heads, tails, and legs partly or completely into their shells.

Many turtles have black, brown, or green shells with a pattern of spots, stripes, or other marks that help them blend in with their surroundings. This blending in is called camouflage.

Soft Shells

Some kinds of turtles do not have scutes—instead, they have soft, leathery skin covering their shells. They are called softshelled turtles. The world's biggest turtle, the leatherback, is softshelled. Its skin is dotted with small, flat pieces of bone. The leatherback needs a flexible shell like this because it dives very deep in the ocean. A hard shell would be crushed by the force and weight of the water.

Turtle Bites

A turtle does not have any teeth in its mouth. Instead, its mouth has sharp edges. A turtle's mouth is so sharp and strong that it is often called a beak. A turtle can cut and tear food into smaller pieces with its beak.

Some kinds of turtles have a hard ridge in their mouth that helps them crush plants or the shells of snails and shellfish. The wide jaws of some turtles also help them to crush strong shells.

Turtle Necks

Turtles that can pull their heads into their shells are called hidden-necked turtles. A hidden-necked turtle bends its neck into a U-shape as it yanks in its head. Its skin then folds up around its head to form a collar. This collar is the reason behind the name "turtleneck" for a high-necked shirt or sweater!

Turtles that cannot pull in their heads are called side-necked turtles. A side-necked turtle twists its head and neck sideways to tuck them into its shell.

The longest necks belong to the snake-necked turtles. Some kinds of snake-necked turtles have necks more than half as long as their shells!

The scutes (tough coverings) on the legs of this turtle give it extra protection. Any predator going for the turtle's pulled-in head will have to get past these sturdy "shields."

Snappers!

Snapping turtles are named after their ability to bite quickly—and hard! A big alligator snapping turtle can even crack a broom handle in two with its jaws!

Turtles that have claws, like this yellow-bellied slider, use them to climb onto logs and rocks and to tear their food into smaller pieces.

Turtle Toes

A turtle's legs and feet are clues to where the turtle lives. Turtles that live in freshwater (nonsalty water) have toes with clawlike nails. Often these toes are webbed like a duck's foot. When the turtle pushes its foot backward in the water, the web spreads wide to form a paddle. It closes up to help the turtle pull its foot forward again easily.

Turtles that live on land have clublike feet that look a bit like an elephant's. The toes seem to be buried in the feet, with only their tough nails sticking out. Many land turtles have scutes (tough shields) on their legs to help protect them. They put their sturdy front legs in front of their face as a shield.

A turtle that lives in the sea has legs that are shaped for a life of swimming. Its front legs are long flippers. A sea turtle "flies" through the water as it paddles with its front legs. It steers with its hind legs. Sea turtles have one or two claws on each flipper, except for the leatherback, which has none.

Chapter 3
Types of Turtles

The spotted turtle lives in swamps, streams, and rivers in the eastern United States and part of Canada. Its top shell is black with lots of small yellow spots. Its legs, neck, tail, and head are polka-dotted too.

Alligator Snappers

The alligator snapper can grow to be more than 2 feet long. The biggest one ever seen weighed 220 pounds—about as much as a newborn baby elephant! An alligator snapper has a pink flap on its tongue that looks something like a worm. It wiggles this "worm" to lure fish into its jaws!

Types of Turtles

There are about 250 kinds of turtles. Most are freshwater turtles that live in water that is not salty—in ponds, marshes, swamps, streams, and lakes. Some other kinds can also live in water that is partly salty. About forty types of turtles live only on land. Some even live in deserts! Just seven kinds live their whole lives in the ocean. They are called sea turtles.

Spotted Turtles

Spotted turtles are freshwater turtles. They spend most of their time in the water, but they often come out to creep through thick patches of plants on shore. Like other freshwater turtles, they also climb onto rocks and logs to bask in the sun.

Snapping Turtles

The snapping turtle is a freshwater turtle with a big, powerful bite. There are two kinds of snappers—the common snapper and the alligator snapper.

The common snapper lives in parts of North America, Central America, and South America. Snappers often lie buried in mud with just their eyes and nostrils sticking out.

The alligator snapper lives in parts of the southeastern and central United States.

The Galapagos Tortoise

The Galapagos (pronounced *guh LAH puh guhs*) are a chain of islands in the Pacific Ocean west of Ecuador. The word *galápago* means "saddle" in Spanish. Some of the huge tortoises (pronounced *TORE tuh sis*) that live on these islands have saddlelike shells. The sailors who discovered these islands in the 1500s named them after the humongous tortoises they found there.

The Galapagos tortoise is a giant among land turtles. A male can measure 6 feet long from nose to tail and weigh up to 600 pounds—about as much as four or five adult humans!

Galapagos tortoises eat grass, leaves, flowers, fruit, and cactuses. Their big bodies can store a lot of water, which helps them survive during dry seasons.

There are about twelve kinds of Galapagos tortoises that live on the islands. Each kind is different from the others in some way. Tortoises that live in places with lots of grass have high, rounded shells. Tortoises living in drier places have longer necks so they can stretch up to eat tall plants. These tortoises have a scoop shape at the front of their top shell that allows them to raise their neck even higher.

Turtle or Tortoise?

When is a turtle a tortoise? In the United States, turtles that live in water are called turtles, but turtles that live on land are called tortoises. Turtles that divide their time between land and water are called terrapins.

The Galapagos tortoise is famous for living a very long life. One of these tortoises lived to the age of 170 years!

Whew!
The desert tortoise can live in an area where the temperature can reach up to 140 degrees F. Maybe that's why this tortoise spends most of the day in its burrow.

A desert tortoise digs burrows with its clunky front legs, which are flatter than its hind legs.

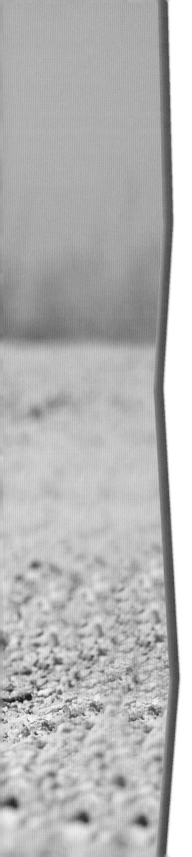

The Desert Tortoise

The desert tortoise can be found in dry areas in the southwestern United States and part of Mexico. Its legs are thick and stumpy.

The desert tortoise crawls across the sand to look for food early in the morning and late in the day. It eats grass and takes bites out of moist cactuses. Cactus fruit is a special treat.

The desert tortoise depends on plants not only for food but also for shelter. It ducks into patches of shade under plants while hunting for food. For the hottest part of the day, it digs a burrow under a plant and stays inside this cool, damp hideaway.

The Leatherback Turtle

The leatherback is the world's largest turtle. This sea turtle can grow to be nearly 8 feet long—about the size of a large sofa. It can weigh about 1,600 pounds—almost as much as a big workhorse! It is named for its leathery top shell, which does not have any scutes, or tough shields.

The leatherback swims faster and dives deeper than any other sea turtle. It has huge front flippers and unusual ridges that run the length of its top shell.

Leatherbacks come close to shore only to mate and lay eggs. A female leatherback will swim across an entire ocean to reach its nesting ground, which is the same beach where it hatched.

The Green Turtle

The green turtle is at home in warm ocean waters, where it swims along coasts and feeds on water plants.

But when the time comes to mate or lay eggs, green turtles travel long distances across the seas. They swim to the same beaches where they themselves hatched. For some green turtles, this is a trip of more than a thousand miles!

Male turtles meet and mate with females in the water. They do not come ashore. But a female ready to lay eggs crawls onto the beach at night. There she digs a nest by scooping at the sand with her front flippers. Her work sends sand flying in all directions. Then she uses her hind feet to dig a small hole in the scooped-out area.

The female lays up to 200 round eggs that look like golf balls. Then she covers the nest and pats down the sand before returning to the sea. The eggs hatch about two months later, and the baby turtles crawl into the water right away.

The Painted Turtle

The painted turtle is one of the most common turtles in the United States. Painted turtles live in ponds, lakes, and other freshwater places with muddy bottoms. You might see one basking in the sun on a log or a rock.

The green turtle is one of only seven kinds of sea turtles in the world.

Tremendous Turtle
The biggest turtle that ever lived was called *Archelon*, a prehistoric sea turtle. *Archelon* was about 12 feet long—as long as four yardsticks placed end to end.

Chapter 4
A Turtle's Life

Turtles can see in color, and red seems to be a favorite shade. Turtles love eating tomatoes and strawberries, and desert tortoises gobble up the red fruits of cactuses. Zookeepers often hide medicine for turtles in juicy red tomatoes!

Turtle Meals

Most turtles are omnivores (pronounced *OM nih vorz*), which means they eat both plants and animals.

Green sea turtles eat grassy plants that grow underwater. They feed on these grasses so much that one kind of plant is called turtle grass. Land turtles eat grass too. They also eat the soft parts of other plants, such as leaves and flowers, and mushrooms. Turtles that live in deserts feed on cactuses. Fruit is always a favorite meal for turtles.

Animal food eaten by turtles includes worms, snails, slugs, insects, and even snakes. In the water, turtles catch and eat snails, minnows, tadpoles, and fish. Most turtles also feed on any dead animals they find.

Thirsty Turtles

A tortoise that lives in a dry habitat is often thirsty. It survives these dry times by storing water in its body and not urinating. If it comes across a puddle, or if it should rain, the tortoise will finally go to the bathroom and drink a lot of water all at once. This water replaces the stored water in its body. A desert tortoise may gulp down as much as a third of its weight in water after a long dry spell!

A Day in the Sun

Because turtles are cold-blooded, their behavior often shows whether they want to warm up or cool down.

A turtle's day usually begins with a warm-up activity! In the early morning, the turtle comes out from its nighttime hiding place. This spot may be a burrow, a pond floor, or a pile of leaves. The turtle moves to a rock or log in a patch of sunlight where it then sits, soaking up heat. This is called basking.

If the turtle gets too hot, it moves to a cooler place. For a freshwater turtle, this may mean just slipping back into the water. For a desert turtle, it means finding and hiding under a shrub or in a burrow, where it is dark and cool.

Surviving Winter

Turtles that live where winter is cold survive by hibernating. A turtle getting ready to hibernate slows down day by day. It eats less as the days grow shorter and cooler. It also goes into a hiding place that will keep it safe from both freezing temperatures and predators. Eventually its heart rate drops and it breathes very slowly. It does not eat, drink, or go to the bathroom all winter.

A box turtle digs a hole for itself. It sleeps away the winter buried about 12 inches underground. Some turtles move into old burrows dug by other animals. A freshwater turtle may bury itself in the mud at the bottom of a pond.

Most turtles don't like company. But when it comes to basking in the sun, they're willing to share a crowded log or rock.

Breathing Underwater
How can a turtle that hibernates underwater get oxygen without coming up for air? The turtle soaks up oxygen from the water through areas of skin in its throat and under its tail. In this way, it gets just enough oxygen to stay alive while it is underwater and nearly motionless.

Chapter 5
Turtles in the World

There were about 250,000 giant tortoises living on the Galapagos Islands before humans discovered them. Now there are about 20,000. The government of Ecuador, scientists, and others are working hard to preserve these gentle giants.

Turtles in Danger

The first turtles lived on Earth at the same time as the dinosaurs—about 200 million years ago. All the dinosaurs died out about 65 million years ago, but the turtles survived. Today, however, many kinds of turtles are in danger of becoming extinct.

Some types of turtles are endangered because their habitats have been damaged. Turtles living in rain forests lose their homes when the trees are cut down. Pond turtles die out when wetlands, such as swamps and marshes, are drained to make way for buildings. Land tortoises are killed when people drive carelessly or cause fires that burn their habitat. Many beaches used by sea turtles for laying eggs have been turned into vacation areas.

Other types of turtles have suffered from being hunted too much. Thousands and thousands of giant tortoises living on islands were killed for food by the crews of old sailing ships. Green turtles have also been heavily hunted, and their eggs have been collected as food. Hawksbill turtles were almost wiped out because people wanted to make combs and other decorations from their shells. Sea turtles are endangered by nets that are used to catch fish and other sea creatures for food. The turtles get caught and are killed accidentally. Turtles are also threatened by pollution and by hunters collecting them from the wild to sell as pets.

The Future of Turtles

Some kinds of turtles live in just one area or one country. They can be helped by people who live in that area or country. Other turtles, such as sea turtles, live worldwide. They need the help of many people and many countries.

One important agreement signed by many nations in 1973 is the Convention on International Trade in Endangered Species. This agreement protects many types of turtles and controls how they may be used. In 1994, many countries also agreed to protect sea turtles.

Groups of volunteers are also making a big difference for turtles. Neighborhoods work to clean up beaches so that garbage doesn't get into the water and harm turtles. People also help protect the nests of sea turtles from predators.

Fast Facts About Painted Turtles

Scientific name	*Chrysemys picta*
Class	Reptilia
Order	Testudines
Size	4 to 9 inches long
Habitat	Streams, rivers, lakes, ponds, marshes

Thanks to the efforts of people and governments working together, this newly hatched turtle—and others like it—can look forward to living a long life in a safe habitat.

Glossary of Wild Words

basking   lying in the sun and soaking up heat

camouflage   colors and patterns on an animal that help it blend in with its surroundings

carapace   the top part of a turtle's shell

cold-blooded   having a body temperature that changes with the animal's habitat

endangered   a specific type of plant or animal in danger of extinction

freshwater   water that is not salty

habitat   the natural environment where an animal or plant lives

hibernate   to go into a deep sleep all winter

omnivore	an animal that eats both plants and meat	**scutes**	the tough, protective shields on a turtle's shell
plastron	the bottom part of a turtle's shell	**species**	a group of living things that are the same in many ways
predator	an animal that hunts and eats other animals to survive	**terrapin**	a turtle that divides its time between living on land and living in water
prey	animals that are hunted by other animals for food		
reptile	a cold-blooded animal	**tortoise**	a turtle that lives on land
		turtle	a reptile with a shell

Index